First World War
and Army of Occupation
War Diary
France, Belgium and Germany

52 DIVISION
Divisional Troops
410 Field Company Royal Engineers
1 April 1918 - 31 May 1919

WO95/2893/1

The Naval & Military Press Ltd
www.nmarchive.com
Published in association with The National Archives

Published by

The Naval & Military Press Ltd

Unit 10 Ridgewood Industrial Park,
Uckfield, East Sussex,
TN22 5QE England
Tel: +44 (0) 1825 749494

www.naval-military-press.com
www.nmarchive.com

This diary has been reprinted in facsimile from the original. Any imperfections are inevitably reproduced and the quality may fall short of modern type and cartographic standards.

© **Crown Copyright**
Images reproduced by permission of The National Archives, London, England, 2015.

Contents

Document type	Place/Title	Date From	Date To
Heading	WO95/2893-1		
Heading	52nd Division 410th (Lowland) Fld Coy R.E Apr 1918-May 1919		
Heading	52nd Divisional Engineers Disembarked Marseilles From Egypt 170418 410th (Lowland) Filed Company R.E April 1918		
War Diary	Hadral	01/04/1918	01/04/1918
War Diary	Sarona	02/04/1918	03/04/1918
War Diary	Surafend	04/04/1918	06/04/1918
War Diary	Kantara	07/04/1918	08/04/1918
War Diary	Alexandria	09/04/1918	10/04/1918
War Diary	At Sea	11/04/1918	16/04/1918
War Diary	Marseilles	17/04/1918	19/04/1918
War Diary	On Train	20/04/1918	21/04/1918
War Diary	Noyelles	22/04/1918	22/04/1918
War Diary	Wattiehurt	23/04/1918	29/04/1918
War Diary	Aire	30/04/1918	30/04/1918
Heading	War Diary 410th (Lowland) Field Co. RE From 1st May 1918 To 31st May 1918 Vol IV No 5		
War Diary	Aire	01/05/1918	01/05/1918
War Diary	Nieppe Wood	02/05/1918	06/05/1918
War Diary	Aire	07/05/1918	07/05/1918
War Diary	Aux Reitz And Forward Camp (bois De Bonval)	08/05/1918	15/05/1918
War Diary	Aux Reitz	16/05/1918	31/05/1918
Heading	War Diary Of 410th (Lowland) Field Co R.E. For Period 1st June 1918 To 30th June 1918		
War Diary	Aux Rietz	01/06/1918	30/06/1918
Heading	War Diary 410 (Low) Field Coy R.E.		
Heading	War Diary Of 410th (Lowland) Field Co. R.E. For Period 1st July 1918 To 31st July 1918		
War Diary	Aux Rietz	01/07/1918	21/07/1918
War Diary	Aux Rietz to Olhain	22/07/1918	30/07/1918
War Diary	Rollincourt	31/07/1918	31/07/1918
Heading	War Diary 410th (Lowland) Field Co.R.E. For Period 1st August 1918 To 31st August 1918 Volume IV No 8		
War Diary	Roclincourt	01/08/1918	17/08/1918
War Diary	Caucourt	18/08/1918	20/08/1918
War Diary	Habarcq	21/08/1918	22/08/1918
War Diary	Barly	23/08/1918	23/08/1918
War Diary	Map 51b SW 52.b.0.8	24/08/1918	25/08/1918
War Diary	Map 51b S.W 54 B 5 6	26/08/1918	27/08/1918
War Diary	Map 51b S W. 52 B 0.8	28/08/1918	30/08/1918
War Diary	Map 51b S.W T 5a 05, 05 Henin Hill	31/08/1918	31/08/1918
Heading	War Diary 410th (Lowland) Field Co R.E. From 1st Aug 1918 Till 31st Aug 1918 Vol IV		
Heading	War Diary 410th (Lowland) Field Coy R.E. For Period 1st Sept 1918 To 30th Sept 1918 Volume IV		
War Diary	Map France 51 B S W Henin Hill	01/09/1918	01/09/1918
War Diary	U 19d 8 8.	01/09/1918	01/09/1918
War Diary	T4 C 6 2 & Bullecourt	02/09/1918	02/09/1918

War Diary	Map France 1:20000 57 C NW	03/09/1918	03/09/1918
War Diary	C4 Central	03/09/1918	06/09/1918
War Diary	B12d8.8	07/09/1918	11/09/1918
War Diary	Map France 1:20000 57 C.N.W.	12/09/1918	12/09/1918
War Diary	B 12d 8.8 & C12c	12/09/1918	12/09/1918
War Diary	C 12c	13/09/1918	17/09/1918
War Diary	Map France 1:20000 57 C NE	17/09/1918	30/09/1918
Heading	War Diary 410th (Lowland) Field Co RE Sep 1918 Vol IV No 9		
Heading	War Diary Of 410th (Lowland) Field Coy RE For Period 1st October 1918 To 31st October 1918 Volume IV		
War Diary	Graincourt	01/10/1918	01/10/1918
War Diary	Cantaing	02/10/1918	06/10/1918
War Diary	Beaumetz Les Cambrai	07/10/1918	08/10/1918
War Diary	Sars Le Bois	09/10/1918	21/10/1918
War Diary	Douai	22/10/1918	23/10/1918
War Diary	Marchiennes	24/10/1918	30/10/1918
War Diary	Lecelles	31/10/1918	31/10/1918
Heading	War Diary 410th (Lowland) Field Co RE 1st-31st Oct 1918 Vol IV		
Heading	War Diary 410th (Lowland) Field Co R.E. From 1/11/1918 To 30/11/1918		
War Diary	Lecelles	01/11/1918	04/11/1918
War Diary	La Vieille Eglise	05/11/1918	08/11/1918
War Diary	Hergnies	09/11/1918	09/11/1918
War Diary	Blaton	10/11/1918	12/11/1918
War Diary	Jurbise	13/11/1918	30/11/1918
Heading	War Diary Of 410th (Lowland) Field Co RE From 1st December 1918 To 31st December 1918		
War Diary	Jurbise (Belgium)	01/12/1918	12/12/1918
War Diary	Lens (Belgium)	14/12/1918	31/12/1918
Heading	410 Field Coy RE War Diary December 1918		
Heading	War Diary Of 410th (Lowland) Field Company RE From Jan 1st 1919 To Jan 31st 1919		
War Diary	Lens (Belgium)	01/01/1919	31/01/1919
Heading	War Diary 410 Fd Coy February 1919 Vol 11		
War Diary	Lens (Belgium)	01/02/1919	28/02/1919
Heading	410 Field Co RE War Diary March 1919 Vol 12		
War Diary	Lens (Belgium)	01/03/1919	22/03/1919
War Diary	Soignies (Belgium)	23/03/1919	31/03/1919
Heading	410 Fd Coy War Diary 1st April 1919 Vol 13		
War Diary	Soignies	01/04/1919	30/04/1919
Heading	War Diary 410 Fd Co R.E. Month Of April 1919		
Heading	410th (Lowland) Field Coy RE War Diary May 1919		
War Diary	Soignies	01/05/1919	31/05/1919

most/2893(1)

most/2893(1)

52ND DIVISION

410TH (LOWLAND) FLD COY R.E.

APR 1918 - MAY 1919

52nd Divisional Engineers

Disembarked MARSEILLES from EGYPT 17.4.18.

410th (Lowland) FIELD COMPAnY R. E.

APRIL 1918.

Army Form C. 2118.

Sheet No. 1

WAR DIARY
or
INTELLIGENCE SUMMARY.
(Erase heading not required.)

Place	Date	Hour	Summary of Events and Information	Remarks and references to Appendices
Hadra.	1st April		RE. work handed over to 4th (Indian) Div. RE; B.C. Tools for 202 Battery R.G.A completed. Shell slits for 380 Heavy Batty. completed. No.2 Section working on Wire Road. Casualties, 1 O.R. admitted to hospital. Weather - showery and cool.	
Sarona.	2nd "		Company moved to Sarona at 0800. Casualties, nil. Weather, very fine.	
Sarona.	3rd "		Kit inspection. Moved to camp N. of Surafend, arriving at 2400. Lt. Sandes went ahead to fix site of camp. Casualties, 1 native driver. Reinforcements, 2 O.R. Weather, very fine.	
Surafend.	4th "		Respirators tested with tear gas. Baggage taken to station. Lieut. Sandes & 2 O.R. leave for Alexandria to obtain 6 fontoons and 3 Trestles. Casualties, nil. Weather, very fine.	
Surafend.	5th "		Returned all vehicles except 8 tool carts, all horses and animals. Seven native drivers returned to A.M.T.D.; Lcpl. Casualties, nil. Weather, fine.	
Surafend.	6th "		Rifle inspection. Left for Kantara by 2351 train. Casualties, nil. Weather, Sunday.	
Kantara.	7th "		Arrived Kantara at 1630. Camped at G.B.D. Reinforcements, 8 O.R. Weather, fine.	
Kantara.	8th "		Lieut. Winship with 30 O.R. leaves for Alexandria with wagons at 0830. Bathing parade. March to Kantara West at 1700 and entrain with 5th Royal Irish Regt. Train starts at 2000. Casualties, nil. Weather, fine.	
Alexandria	9th "		Arrive Sidi Bishr Transit Camp at 0530. Casualties 1 O.R. Reinforcements 1 O.R. Weather, fine.	OP

Army Form C. 2118.
Sheet No 2

WAR DIARY
or
INTELLIGENCE SUMMARY.
(Erase heading not required.)

Place	Date	Hour	Summary of Events and Information	Remarks and references to Appendices
Alexandria to Gabbari	11th		Entrain about 10.00 to Gabbari. No. 45 Quay. Lieuts. Winshill and Sarolea with 4.9 O.R. plus 2 O.R. of 4/2 Fd Coy. R.E. and all wagons on board S.S. "Indarra". Lieuts Hancock & Graham Brown with mounted section, 52 O.R. on board S.S. "Caledonia". Remainder of Coy., 125 O.R. plus 3 attached on board S.S. "Osmond". Casualties, nil. Weather, fine.	
At Sea.	12th "		Move to mts. harbour and bank. Move out at 14.00. Casualties, nil. Weather, fine.	
" "	13th "		Fine weather but choppy sea. Casualties, nil.	
" "	14th "		Fine weather and smooth sea. Casualties, nil.	
" "	15th "		Fine weather but rather choppy sea. Casualties, nil.	
" "	16th "		Fine weather, fairly rough sea in evening. Casualties, nil.	
" "	16th "		Weather, fine throughout, smooth sea. Casualties, 1 O.R. to hospital.	
Marseilles.	17th "		Arrived Marseilles about 07.30. Lieuts. Winshill & Sarolea with 49 O.R. remained on board "Indarra", remainder of Company went to No. 10 Rest Camp. Casualties, nil. Weather, fine early but not later.	
"	18th "		Company gone down to docks and unloaded horses and trailers & wagons. Casualties, nil. Weather showery.	
"	19th "		Company left camp at 09.00 for station and loaded wagons in train. Company, less Lieut Winshill & 110 O.R., entrained at 16.20 leaving shortly afterwards. Lieut Winshill and party followed in next train at 22.00. Reinforcements sent for missing R.E. Horses. Weather, fine.	[1]

410th (COWLEY) FIELD COMPANY
No. 17 April 1918
ROYAL ENGINEERS

Army Form C. 2118.

Sheet No 3

WAR DIARY
or
INTELLIGENCE SUMMARY.
(Erase heading not required.)

Instructions regarding War Diaries and Intelligence Summaries are contained in F.S. Regs., Part II. and the Staff Manual respectively. Title pages will be prepared in manuscript.

Place	Date	Hour	Summary of Events and Information	Remarks and references to Appendices
On Train	20th Apl		Arrived at Le Hd about 0745 and remained there for about an hour. Wet weather. Casualties, nil.	
"	21st "		Halted at Pernes-le-Promiel. Wet morning, fine later. Casualties, nil.	
Royelles	22nd "		Detrained at Royelles at 1100. Lieut Wandell's party detained at 1200. Company and transport left Royelles arriving Witherhurst at 1700 and billeted. Reinforcements 20 R. rejoined from 52nd Div RE. Held 7.8. Casualties nil. Wet morning, fine late.	
Witherhurst	23rd "		Rit inspection, 9no and musketry drill. Casualties Nil.	
"	24th "		Work as yesterday including route march in morning. Bayjcks and transport drawn. Gas Bayonet and musketry instructor temporarily attached. Casualties nil. Weather fine and cold.	
"	25th "		Weather fine. Work as yesterday including turn-out at 3rd Army Rest Camp. Pay. Gas Bay. & fighting & the Musketry Instructs. attached. Casualties Nil.	
"	26 "		Weather Fine. Work as yesterday including night practice laying out trenches. Casualties nil.	
"	27" "		Weather Fine. Work as usual. Straw riding horses & balance of draught horses. Rifle practice for NCO. Company in Pneumatic Symptoms. Casualties, 2 OTR admitted to hospital.	

Army Form C. 2118.

Sheet No. 4

WAR DIARY
or
INTELLIGENCE SUMMARY.
(Erase heading not required.)

410th (LOWLAND) FIELD COMPANY ROYAL ENGINEERS

Place	Date	Hour	Summary of Events and Information	Remarks and references to Appendices
Walheim	28*		Weather showery. Work as usual.	
	29*	04.00	Reveille. 06.30 Company left Walheim and entrained 12.15 from left Nopelle. 06.30 Coy. arr. at Nopelle Station and marched to Aire. 19.30 detrained at Bergette and Guoughs in Billeted at the 1st Army Artillery School Barroda, Caurelli.	Photographs of work left.
Aire	30*		Training as usual. Weather fair.	

No. 2

CONFIDENTIAL

WAR DIARY

H10th (Lowland) Field Co. R.E.

from 1st May 1918
till 31st May 1918

Vol IV   No 5

WAR DIARY or INTELLIGENCE SUMMARY

Army Form C. 2118.

410 (2nd) Field RE

Place	Date MAY	Hour	Summary of Events and Information	Weather	Remarks and references to Appendices
AIRE	1.	0830	Company moved to NIEPPE WOOD for duty with 5th Division on Divisional line.	Fine	
NIEPPE WOOD	2		Wiring Divisional line from North Side of NIEPPE WOOD, behind LE PARC and up to left of Divisional Boundary.	Fine	
Do.	3		Work as yesterday.	Fine	
Do	4		Work as yesterday.	Fine	
Do	5		Work as yesterday. Lieut Scoular and 1 O.R. got forward with 155 Bde. party to arrange billets Reinforcement. 1 O.R.	Rain & Thunder	
Do	6"	0830	Dismounted ranks moved to AIRE, into billets at Artillery Barracks (155 Bde. Pioneer Coy. under Lieut Graham, Brown and Mounted section with Transport proceed by road to DIVION Lieut. B Winship accompanies C.R.E. to take over from 400th Fld. Coy. at AUX REITZ.	Fine	
AIRE	7d	2000	Company training in knots, lashings & Anti-gas measures. Company (Dismounted section) entrained at AIRE with 155 Bde Pioneer Coy. for MARSEUIL. Mounted section & Transport proceed by road from DIVION and arrive at AUX REITZ about 1530. Sick To Hosp 3. O.R.	WET	

Army Form C. 2118.

420 (2nd) Field Co RE WAR DIARY or INTELLIGENCE SUMMARY.
(Erase heading not required.)

Instructions regarding War Diaries and Intelligence Summaries are contained in F. S. Regs., Part II. and the Staff Manual respectively. Title pages will be prepared in manuscript.

Place	Date n14Y	Hour	Summary of Events and Information	Remarks and references to Appendices
AUX REITZ and FORWARD CAMP (Bois de Boman)	8TH	0500	Arrived at MAROEUIL and marched Sappers to AUX REITZ camp. Pioneer Coy carries another camp. Took over works from 400' Field Coy RE (51st Div) comprising:- Improvements to trenches, resiting and duckboarding. Construction of Bn. Dugouts. Running Engine for Elec. Electric lighting plant, Boiler pump at Betta, Watertrolley gate at R.E. Dump Zine. Work on Road Minas Nos 6 & 7.	Fine
		2000	Lieut. Worthly & Sanders with Section Nos 1 & 2 take over forward camp & works in line. Hosp. Sick. 1 O.R.	Fine
Do: Do:	9th		Work as yesterday in addition of 5th R. Innisk Bnstn (Pioneers) working on Green Line near Thelus. Superintendence of Dugout construction stopped ˗ reserve trench work is more important. Hosp. Sick. 2 O.R.	Fine
Do: Do:	10th		Work as yesterday including instruction in Lewis Gun.	Fine
Do: Do:	11th		Work as yesterday. All spare sappers assist Pioneers on Elsdon Post and wiring of Toned alley trench. (Span to Test Box (Signal) T 25 d 32.	Fine
Do: Do:	12th		Worked as yesterday. Test Box completed. Bde Armourer examines & repairs Coy rifles Hosp. Sick. 1 O.R.	Fine
Do: Do:	13th		Worked as yesterday. Armourer completes Coy rifles & takes up Pioneer Coy rifles.	RAIN

410 (Lowo) Field Co. E **WAR DIARY**

or

INTELLIGENCE SUMMARY.

(Erase heading not required.)

Army Form C. 2118.

Place	Date MAY.	Hour	Summary of Events and Information	Remarks and references to Appendices
CAMPS at AUX REITZ and BOIS de BONVAL	14.		Work as yesterday.	Fine.
Do: Do:	15.	2000	Work as yesterday, including forward pt at AUX REITZ, and improving FURBUS POST. Forward Section found over BOIS de BONVAL camp and workers to AUX Field Coy RE.	Fine. Hot.
AUX REITZ	16.		Nos 1 & 2 Sections start intensive training. Other PIONEER Fata over AUX 2nd GHQ works on yesterday. No 3 & 4 Section works on BROWN LINE (N of WHITE.) Hosp:- Sick 2 O.R. Dental 2 O.R.	do do
Do:	17		Work as yesterday. Hosp:- Sick 5 O.R.	do do
Do:	18		Work as yesterday including 1 NCO. & 6 OR. recruiting at D.H.Q. Field Workshop. 1 NCO. and Batman posted to 18th Corps Anti Gas School FRESSIN. Drum & trumpeters attached to C.R.E.'s staff. Hosp:- Dental 2 O.R.	do do
Do:	19.		Work as yesterday including Elephant Shelters (small) fixed in BROWN LINE (night work) attached to 1st Canadian Tunnelling Coy. for work on Dugouts. 155 Bde Pioneer Coy. in line from this date Hosp: Sick 1 O.R. Rejoined :- 2. O.R.	do do
Do:	20.		Work as yesterday.	do do
Do:	21.		Work as yesterday. New Signal Dugout for D.H.Q. Repairs to Aid Post A.11.d.39. No 2 Section cease training. Recruiting complete at D.H.Q. de do Hosp: Dental 1 O.R. Rejoined 1. O.R.	

4/O (Can) Field C.R.E.

WAR DIARY
or
INTELLIGENCE SUMMARY.
(Erase heading not required.)

Army Form C. 2118.

Place	Date	Hour	Summary of Events and Information	Remarks and references to Appendices	Weather
AUX RIETZ	22nd		Work as yesterday, including 3 Sappers repairing at BERTHONVAL GATES: No1 Section dug slits fr Mountill Sect & provide men protection for horses in stabling. Lt BEATTIE R.E. joined R.A. Hospl: Sick 1.O.R. Rejoined 1.O.R.		Fine
Do.	23rd		Work as yesterday. Lieut Graham Brown commenced survey fr improvements to FRAZER & OTTAWA camps. 1 N.C.O. and 6 O.R. on repairs at Convent Ave & D.H.Q. & G.O.C. stables.		Windy & cloudy
Do.	24th		No1 & 2 Sections commence work on BROWN LINE in front of VIMY. No.3 commence training. Sunday jobs as before.		Wet
Do.	25th		Nos 3 & 4 Sec Training. Commenced Gasproof Hut at St Eloi. Other jobs as yesterday. Lieut Duncan taken up Road Reconnaisance for R.A. Rejoined 1 O.R.		Fine
Do.	26th		No 4 Sec. Training. Other jobs as yesterday, including Camofage of Johnathan. Gun line finishes Sections ploughed plot at back of stables. Lieut Winship I NCO + 6 OR men at Gen Connell.		Fine
Do.	27		Training Ceases. No 4 Sec. commence improvements at Frazer + Ottawa camps with Lieut. Graham Brown. Other work as yesterday.		Fine
Do.	28		Work as yesterday. Gasshit Pt. Eloi completed. Lieut Hancock surveys R.A. Dugouts for delapidations on gasproof curtains. Survey for accommodation in AUX RIETZ — Zivy CAVES. Hosp: Sick 1.O.R.		Fine
Do.	29		All works as yesterday; including an artillery Bridge over Jonathan. Lieut Graham Brown and 15 men improving Frazer + Ottawa Camps and taken over by Col. Crocke. C.R.E. 1st Corps for works from this day. Hosp. Sick 2 O.R.		Fine

40 (Jew) Field Co. RE

WAR DIARY
or
INTELLIGENCE SUMMARY.
(Erase heading not required.)

Army Form C. 2118.

Place	Date MAY	Hour	Summary of Events and Information	Weather	Remarks and references to Appendices
AUX REITZ	30.		Works as yesterday, including 5 O.R. preparing gas curtains for R.A. Dugouts, also preparation of incendiary charges for HOOPER'S DUMP, and repair to Concrete Hut at Frezen Camp. Hosp:- Sick. 1. O.R. Reinforcements. 1. O.R.	Fine	
	31."		Works as yesterday, including splinter proof protection to Huts in Frezen Camp & own Eng. Billets at AUX REITZ	Fine	

R.D. Hutton Major R.E.
O.C. 40 Field Co. R.E.
1.6.18.

CONFIDENTIAL.

WAR DIARY

of

410th (LOWLAND) FIELD Co., R.E.

for Period

1st June 1918 to 30th June 1918

Volume

410th Lowl. Fd. Coy. R.E. **WAR DIARY** or **INTELLIGENCE SUMMARY.**
JUNE 1918
(Erase heading not required.)

Army Form C. 2118.

Place	Date	Hour	Summary of Events and Information	WEATHER	Remarks and references to Appendices
AUX RIETZ	1st.		WORK on Improving Reserve Area Ruffels; Brown Line: New Main Dressing Station at ST. ELOY (MAROEUIL 1:20000 F.9.c.7.4.). Gas proofing R.A. dugouts for IX Bde. R.F.A. Improving Fd. Coy. Stables. Digging round huts in Fraser Camp. Re-erecting huts for C.R.E. 2/Lt Hindson 1/4.R.S.F. reports for Pioneer Coy. 1 O.R. revert.	Fine.	
Do.	2nd.		Sunday. WORK as yesterday. 17th North. Inds. Pr. Bn. in BROWN LINE by night. Bathing Parades. M. Denchar 15 C.E. XVIII CORPS. Casualties NIL	Do.	
Do.	3rd.		WORK as above. Boxing in Trestle wagons. Work on camouflage. Casualties NIL.	Do.	
Do.	4th.		WORK as above. 2/Lt Madlock joins coy and relieves Lt. Graham-Brown who is working in Camps improvement under C.R.E. Corps Troops. Casualties NIL.	Do.	
Do.	5th.		WORK as above. BROWN LINE as usual, also New Dressing Station ST ELOY. Lt. Sancha returns from Leave. 1 O.R. to hosp. sick.	Do.	
Do.	6th.		Improving Reserve Area Ruffels; Erecting Ambulance huts. Gas proofing R.Q. dugouts work in BROWN LINE: Camouflaged ground started FARBUS O.P.: erecting huts for D.T.M.O. Casualties nil.	Do.	[?]

410th FIELD COY. R.E.   JUNE 1918

Army Form C. 2118.

WAR DIARY or INTELLIGENCE SUMMARY.
(Erase heading not required.)

Instructions regarding War Diaries and Intelligence Summaries are contained in F. S. Regs., Part II. and the Staff Manual respectively. Title pages will be prepared in manuscript.

Place	Date	Hour	Summary of Events and Information	Weather	Remarks and references to Appendices
AUX RIETZ	7/6		Work as yesterday. Recon. for FARBUS O.P. at night and camouflaging it. 3 O.R. to hosp. sick. 1 O.R. rejoined.	Fine.	
do.	8/6		Work as yesterday. 3 O.R. to hosp. sick.	do.	
do.	9/6		(Sunday.) Bathing parade. Work as yesterday. THELUS and FARBUS O.P.'s by night. 1 O.R. sick to hosp.	do.	
do.	10/6		Work as yesterday. Also reconn. to NEUVILLE ST. VAAST Baths. 3 O.R. sick to hosp. 1 O.R. rejoined.	8 Sqlt Rcmn.	
do.	11/6		Work as yesterday. 1 O.R. sick to hosp. 4 O.R. from 6.B.D.	Fine.	
do.	12/6		Work as yesterday. Gas proofing dugouts in THELUS POST. Casualties NIL.	do.	
do.	13/6		Work as yesterday. 2/Lt. Medforth and 2 O.R. sick to hosp.	do.	
do.	14/6		Work as yesterday. 5 O.R. sick to hosp. 1 re rejoined.	do.	
do.	15/6		New dugouts Sh. ST. ELOY. Gas proofing dugouts THELUS POST. Work on THELUS and FARBUS O.P.'s. R.F.A. dugouts, improving Billets Reserve Bd. Area. 1 O.R. to hosp. sick.	do.	
do.	16/6		(Sunday.) Work as yesterday. Bathing parade. 2 O.R. to hosp. sick.	Showery.	

Army Form C. 2118.

WAR DIARY
or
INTELLIGENCE SUMMARY.
(Erase heading not required.)

410TH FIELD COY R.E.   JUNE 1918.   (3)

Place	Date	Hour	Summary of Events and Information	Weather	Remarks and references to Appendices
AUX RIETZ	17th		Work as yesterday, also started work on a new Dug out hi NEUVILLE- ST. VAAST also Bomb proofing horse lines. 6 OR to hosp. sick.	fine.	
do.	18th		Work as above. Casualties nil.	fine, cloudy.	
do.	19th		Work as above also repairing CAMPBELL ROAD. 1 OR sick to hosp.	fine.	
do.	20th		Work as above. 3 OR reinf. 1 OR returned.	do.	
do.	21st		Work as above. finished repairs Campbell Road. Work on M.G. Bn's camp. 1 OR reinf. 2 OR returned	showery.	
do.	22nd		Work as above. 1 OR reinf.	do.	
do.	23rd		Work as above. also camouflage by night. 1 OR sick. 10 R. reinf.	fine.	
do.	24th		Work as above. Bathing parades. 1 OR sick. 2 OR reinf.	wet.	
do.	25th		Work as above. 3 OR reinf.	fine.	

410th Field Coy. R.E. WAR DIARY or INTELLIGENCE SUMMARY.

Army Form C. 2118.

June.

Place	Date	Hour	Summary of Events and Information	Weather	Remarks and references to Appendices
Aux R.1672	26th		New Dressing Stn: THELUS and FARBUS O.P's.; BROWN LINE: Disinfestor at NEUVILLE ST VAAST. Baths: R.A. dugouts: improving billets ST ELOY. Bomb proofing horse lines: work in M.G. Bn. Camp. Camouflage work by night. 2 O.R. reinf.	Fine.	
Do.	27th		work as yesterday. Casualties Nil.	Do.	
Do.	28th		work as above. Casualties Nil.	Do.	
Do.	29th		work as above. Platform at ST ELOY. Casualties Nil.	Do.	
Do.	30th		Sunday work as above. Bathing parade. Casualties Nil.	Do.	

P. Whittier Major
O.C. 410 Fd Coy.
1.7.18

Confidential

War Diary
410 (Howr)
Field Coy RE

Vol 4

CONFIDENTIAL

WAR DIARY
of
410th (LOWLAND) FIELD CO., R.E.

for Period

1st July 1918 To 31st July, 1918

410th Lond. fd. Coy. R.E.
JULY 1918

WAR DIARY
or
INTELLIGENCE SUMMARY
(Erase heading not required.)

Army Form C. 2118.

Place	Date	Hour	Summary of Events and Information	WEATHER	Remarks and references to Appendices
AUX RIETZ	1st		Work on Main Dressing Station ST. ELOY; work on THELUS O.P.; FARBUS O.P. and dugout; Observator NEUVILLE ST VAAST Baths; work on Battery Positions and deep dugouts for R.F.A.; Billet improvement at ST ELOY; making revetted banks vannol R.F.A horse lines: work on M.G. Bn. camp; making a covered and raised platform for a ration dump at BLACKPOOL SIDING; work on Brown Line. Casualties NIL.	Fine.	
Do.	2nd.		Work as above: also gas proofing test box for SIGNAL COY. 2/Lt. G.T. Medforth and one OR from hospital.	Do.	
Do.	3rd.		Work as above. Billet improvement at MONT ST ELOY and NEUVILLE ST VAAST 1 OR sick to hosp. 1 OR reinforcement.	Do.	
Do.	4th.		Work as above. Gas proofing test box for SIGNAL COY finished. 1 OR reinft.	Do.	
Do.	5th.		Work as above.		1 OR to hosp. Do.
Do.	6th.		Work as above.	1 OR reinft.	Do.
Do.	7th.		Work as above.	1 OR to hosp. 3 OR reinfts.	Do.
Do.	8th.		Work as above. Dumptons at NEUVILLE ST VAAST Baths finished. Casualties nil.	Do.	

410 Lowl. Fd. Coy. R.E.
July 1918

WAR DIARY
or
INTELLIGENCE SUMMARY.
(Erase heading not required.)

Army Form C. 2118.

Place	Date	Hour	Summary of Events and Information	WEATHER.	Remarks and references to Appendices
AUX RIETZ.	9th.		THELUS O.P.; FARBUS O.P.; wiring BROWN LINE; Railway Dump at BLACKPOOL sidings; Mann Dressing Station ST. ELOY; marking & revetted trenches at R.F.A. horse lines; Battery positions and deep dugouts for R.F.A. Improvements to B.a.R. House NEUVILLE ST. VAAST. Repair work in FRONT ST. ELOY and NEUVILLE ST. VAAST. 10 OR reinforcements.	Rain.	
Do	10th.		Work as yesterday. Repairing camouflage near VIMY at mg Pit. 1 OR to hosp.	Do.	
Do	11th.		Work as yesterday. FARBUS O.P. finished; drawing the BROWN LINE 1 OR to hosp. 1 OR reinf.	Fine.	
Do	12th.		Work as yesterday. Casualties NIL.	Do	
Do	13th.		Work as yesterday; work on Duckwalks ST. ELOY Stand to. 1 OR reinf.	Do	
Do	14th.		Work as yesterday. THELUS O.P. finished. 1 OR to hosp. 1 O.R. reinf.	Do.	
Do	15th.		Work as yesterday; improvements to LATTA camp. 1 OR to hosp. 1 OR reinf.	Rain Do	
Do	16th.		Work as yesterday; also work on pools Whnnd BROWN LINE. making revetments at Railway Dump at LEADLEY sidings; mending trough for M.V.S. Casualties NIL.	Fine Rain.	

Army Form C. 2118.

410 Lowl Fd. Coy, R.E.
JULY 1918

WAR DIARY
or
INTELLIGENCE SUMMARY.
(Erase heading not required.)

Instructions regarding War Diaries and Intelligence Summaries are contained in F. S. Regs., Part II. and the Staff Manual respectively. Title pages will be prepared in manuscript.

Place	Date	Hour	Summary of Events and Information	WEATHER	Remarks and references to Appendices
AUX RIETZ	17th		Works: making a road for O.A.P.O.S.: work on small pools behind BROWN LINE, camp improvement in ST. ELOY; NEUVILLE ST. VAAST and LATTA camp, screening LA TARGETTE ammunition Dump, dirt from a neighbouring coal dump. work on BROWN LINE: work on BLACKPOOL and LEADLEY Rotar Dumps: work on Main Dressing Station ST. ELOY, gun positions and deep dugouts for R.F.A. Promptia at MONT ST ELOY. Casualties NIL.	fine	
do.	18th		Work as yesterday: road for DAPOS finished. Casualties NIL	do.	
do.	19th		Work as yesterday	do.	
do.	20th		Work as yesterday: screen at LA TARGETTE Ammn. dump finished. 1 OR reinft.	thunder showery day	
do.	21st		Bathing parades and inspections. 2 OR reinft.		
AUX RIETZ TO OLHAIN	22nd		Relieved by 490'L Fd. Coy, R.E. 8th Divisn. Moved off 1000 via ST. ELOY CAMBLAIN L'ABBÉ; ESTRÉE CAUCHÉE to OLHAIN arriving about 1500. Men billeted in farms. 3 or reinft.	fine	

410 LOWL. FD. COY. R.E.
JULY 1918

Army Form C. 2118.

WAR DIARY
or
INTELLIGENCE SUMMARY.
(Erase heading not required.)

Instructions regarding War Diaries and Intelligence Summaries are contained in F.S. Regs., Part II. and the Staff Manual respectively. Title pages will be prepared in manuscript.

Place	Date	Hour	Summary of Events and Information	Weather	Remarks and references to Appendices
OLHAIN.	23rd		Training { Kit inspections. Route marches. Physical Training. Drill. Lewis Gun instruction and practice on Range under qualified instructor. Bayonet fighting under qualified instructor. Horse and semaphore. Musketry. Lectures on Field Defence, Demolitions, Bridging, First Aid etc.	fine	
do.	24th			do	
do.	25th			Rain	
do.	26th			do	
do.	27th			do	
do.	28th				
do.	29th				
do.	30th		Work. Making & setting superstructure for water tanks		

CASUALTIES
	23	24	25	26	27	28	29	30
To hosp	1	0	0	1	0	0	1	1
Reenforcts	0	0	0	0	1	2	2	0

| ROCLINCOURT | 31st | | Coy. moved into the line to relieve 10th Bn. C.E. Dismounted men marched to CAMBLAIN L'ABBE and entrained thence for 21VY dump in Light Railway. Mounted Section and cycles moved 0800 by road. Location of Coy. HQrs. MAROEUIL 1:20000 A 28 central (ROCLINCOURT) and nos. 1 and 2 sections. " nos. 3 and 4 " " B 14 central (SPUR POST) " Mtd. Section " " A 13 b central (near AUX RIETZ). Casualties Nil | 31st. | |

CONFIDENTIAL

WAR DIARY
of
410th (LOWLAND) FIELD Co, R.E

for Period

1st August 1918 to 31st August 1918

Volume IV No 8

410th (LOWLAND) FIELD Coy R.E.
Aug. 1918.

WAR DIARY
or
INTELLIGENCE SUMMARY.
(Erase heading not required.)

Army Form C. 2118.

Instructions regarding War Diaries and Intelligence Summaries are contained in F. S. Regs., Part II. and the Staff Manual respectively. Title pages will be prepared in manuscript.

Place	Date	Hour	Summary of Events and Information	Weather	Remarks and references to Appendices
ROCLINCOURT	1st		Nos. 1 & 2 Sections Zawny. No. 3 & 4 Sections as before. All Sections employed on dug outs at work on shelters, keeping up lights & telephone to front line. Drew and transported from dumps GROWN LINE & SUNKEN RD. N. of RŒUX. Burial parties & dumps employed at HYDERABAD REDOUBT. BRIERLEY HILL & inspection of some positions round DUISANS. Repair and repairs to dugouts & shelters on various trenches. Reinforcements 2 O.R.	Fine	
Do.	2nd		Work as above. Making visits and reports to Brigade Engineer.	Fine	
Do.	3rd		Work as above.	wet	
Do.	4th		Work as above.	wet	
Do.	5th		Work as above. Parties for Army Pipe Trains laying O.R's Ballypool to ECURIE.	Wet	
Do.	6th		Work as above.	fine	

H.Q. (Div) Field Co R.E.
AUG 1918

WAR DIARY
or
INTELLIGENCE SUMMARY.
(Erase heading not required.)

Army Form C. 2118.

Place	Date	Hour	Summary of Events and Information	WEATHER	Remarks and references to Appendices
ROCLINCOURT	7th		Work as yesterday. Day's programme complete. 1 O.R. Sick to Hosp.	Fine	
Do	8th		Work as yesterday. Ranking Ramp. Repairs in rutted Boards and Revetting to trench in front THELUS Post, front Batn Hdqtrs.	Fine	
Do	9th		Coy's work consists of Rifle & Lewis Gun Emplacements, wire entg'mts in Boom line and M.G. emp'ts, Bury Line, & Tanker Road 3 BLACK LINES. Dummy emp'ts and ammunition dumps laying. Evacuation of enemy Dug outs & burying note boards; Keeping roads & tracks in repair round THELUS; Defence works, emp'ts, Dug outs & PROGRESS HILL; Construction by Retaining Walls and J.Ref emp'ts on PROGRESS HILL. No 4 & 2. Coys are taking 1 O.R. to Hosp. Sick.		
Do	10th		As yesterday. Enemy shelled vicinity of THELUS Post. Wounded 2 M.T. men belonging to R.F.A. Down in Bivvie & 2 M.G.O.R.s attended but 172 Divisional Cp.	Fine	
Do	11th		As yesterday. 1 Officer & 9 O.R. proceed to First Army Rifle Meeting. 1 O.R. to Hosp. Wounded.	Very fine	1 O.R. to Hosp. Sick.
Do	12th		As yesterday. Reinf. 1 O.R.	Very fine	
Do	13th		As yesterday. Engineer stores being dumped at BRIGADE HILL Divisional Carrying Coys provided labour and Coy. Horses moved from Brigade Enghouse & vicinity.	Fine	R.141/4

470 (Dow) Field Co. R.E.
AUG 1918

WAR DIARY
or
INTELLIGENCE SUMMARY
(Erase heading not required.)

Army Form C. 2118.

Place	Date	Hour	Summary of Events and Information	Weather	Remarks and references to Appendices
ROSSIGNOL	14th		Went on quietly	Very fine	
Do.	15th		Work handed over to 10th Field Coy R.E. 8th Division Btn. Rejoined Company.	Rient. 2 O.R. 1 O.R. To Hosp. Sick	
Do.	16th		Training	1 O.R. To Hosp. Sick	Do.
Do.	17th		Training	22nd June	
			1 Officer & 9 O.R. gone from Third Army Rifle Meeting	Do.	
			Returned from Leave two men. Rejoined from Leave 2nd Cpl. R.E.	To Hosp Sick. 2 O.R.	
CAUCOURT	18th		Company moved to CAUCOURT. Reinf. 2 O.R. Rejoined from Hosp. 1 O.R.	Do.	
Do.	19th		Training — Being Engs. at CAUCOURT Camp.	Do.	
Do.	20th		Reinf. 2 O.R.	Do.	
			Moved to HABARCQ — work — building hutments & M.R. returning by Car in evening	Dull	Reinf. 3 O.R.
HABARCQ	21st		Training & inspection carrying out.	Very fine	
Do.	22nd		Training & testing — Company moved to BARLY at 2 P.M. Rejoined from Hosp. 2 O.R.	Do.	W.B.H.

410 (Dow) Field Coy.
Aug. 1918

WAR DIARY
or
INTELLIGENCE SUMMARY.

Army Form C. 2118.

Place	Date	Hour	Summary of Events and Information	Weather	Remarks and references to Appendices
BARLY	23rd		Remain in QUARTERS at GROSVILLE.	Fine	
	24th		To Hosp. Sick. 2 O.R.		
Map 51B SW 52 6 0.8	24th		Move from GROSVILLE to camp at 52.6.0.8. Remained at BOSIEUX DUMONT and from COJEUL now Bridge ISLAINVILLE. Sent one section to S10 on B4 at S30.33 leaving 11 infantry below.	Fine	
Do	25th		Work on pontoon bridge.	Wet	
			To Hosp. Sick. 2 O.R.		
Map 51B SW 54.65.6	26th		Started at 3.30am to establish Bridge (St Hobert) 2 P.N. of the Regiment wide twenty and must for HINDENBURG LINE (Lt Dunn) Reconnaissance dry ??? & must found Bridge on MEDFORTH side & St Martin information home by N 32 section to N 27 entire complete home by 9pm	Fine	
Do	27th		Work on Lorry. Moved yesterday. NEUVILLE VITASSE - HENIN and HENIN - Bridge now over ANSE CO/JOE at ST MARTIN returned - with recommend to work at HENINEL. extra day returned to camp at 52.6.0.6 at night.	Fine	
			To Hosp Wounded 3 O.R. Sick 1 O.R.		
Map 51B SW 52.6.0.8	28th		Remy	Fine	

410 (Lowland) Field Co RE
AUG. 1918

WAR DIARY
or
INTELLIGENCE SUMMARY.
(Erase heading not required.)

Army Form C. 2118.

Instructions regarding War Diaries and Intelligence Summaries are contained in F. S. Regs., Part II. and the Staff Manual respectively. Title pages will be prepared in manuscript.

(5)

Place	Date	Hour	Summary of Events and Information	Remarks and references to Appendices
Map 51BSW 52.B.0.8.	29		Building temporary huts for 155 Bde HQrs and Battalions. 2 OR. sick to hospital. No. 414055 Cpl J. Donance recommended for immediate award as below. X	
"	30		Repairing road from HENIN in direction of CROISILLES. Working parties to 155 Bde. Making aiming posts and improving T lines for 52 D N 6 Bn.	
Map 51BSW 75 a.05.0.5. HENIN HILL	31st		Coy. moves to HENIN HILL. Reconnaissance of works also made in FONTAINE CROISILLES and Ruin SENSÉE Ry between CROISILLES and FONTAINE LES CROISILLES. 1 OR. wounded. 1 OR. sick to hospital	
			X. No 414055 Cpl John Donance 410th Lowland Field Co RE. HINDENBURG LINE, WEST of HENINEL. On 26.8.18 he was engaged with a party of Sappers in blocking trenches and examining mined dugouts to Kops in the HINDENBURG LINE. Sh. Infantry having their dentist his Neco and Capl Donance offered his assistance. He was of great service to that officer in examining the operation and marking a track in reaching 1st objective. Also when with another infantry party on 27.8.18 engaged in similar work he displayed great courage in entering and examining the HINDENBURG LINE trench ahead of the infantry. He also improved hostile trench work natural terrain on the spot, all the advantages gained being already used the operation. His operation and information used the training throughout had a great effect on the morale of the troops.	

R.D. Chester Major RE
O.C. 410th Fd Co RE
1.9.18.

CONFIDENTIAL

WAR DIARY

410th (Lowland) Field Co. R.E.

from 1st Aug 1918
till 31st Aug 1918

Vol IV No 8

CONFIDENTIAL.

Vol. 6

WAR DIARY.
of
410th (Lowland) Field Coy, R.E.

FOR PERIOD.

1st Sept 1918 To 30th Sept 1918.

VOLUME IV No 9.

#10th (Lowland) Field Co RE.
SEPT 1918

Army Form C. 2118.

WAR DIARY
or
INTELLIGENCE SUMMARY.
(Erase heading not required.)

Instructions regarding War Diaries and Intelligence Summaries are contained in F. S. Regs., Part II. and the Staff Manual respectively. Title pages will be prepared in manuscript.

Place	Date	Hour	Summary of Events and Information	Weather	Remarks and references to Appendices
Map FRANCE 1/20,000 57c.S.W. HENIN HILL	1st		Reconnaissance of roads and wells in and around FONTAINE LES CROISILLES. Remainder of company make a track in dry weather from HENIN HILL to the FONTAINE LES CROISILLES - CROISILLES road. This track was already marked out & rolled by 416 Fd Co RE. In the afternoon, 2/Lt MEDFORTH and 17 men of No 2 section join 6th RSF at BULLECOURT for the purpose of finding entrances in BULLECOURT to the supposed tunnels from that place to FONTAINE, QUÉANT, CROISILLES and SOUTH. Company moves to U19d88. on BULLECOURT-CROISILLES road. Mounted section SEE MC T4 c6.2. Rent 1 O.R.	Fine	
Map FRANCE 1/20,000 57c.S.W. T4 C6.2. & BULLECOURT	2nd		Reconnaissance of roads from BULLECOURT in direction of QUÉANT and for wells in BULLECOURT. Repair of roads in and around BULLECOURT, fixing up pumps at deep wells in BULLECOURT and repairing existing deep well pumps. A large German pioneer dump was found near BULLECOURT and taken over by the Company. 2/Lt MEDFORTH's party search for tunnels as yesterday but none can be found. Mounted Section moves to T23 c7.7. Sick - To Hosp. 1 O.R.	Fine	
Map FRANCE 1/20,000 57c.S.W. C4 central	3rd		QUÉANT occupied by 52 Div. Reconnaissance of road from BULLECOURT to QUÉANT and of wells in QUÉANT and neighbouring hamlets. Making track from BULLECOURT via the HIRONDELLE River Valley at C11 c. B4. (map FRANCE 1/20,000, 57 c.N.W.) to QUÉANT and repairing NOREUIL - QUÉANT road. This was finished by about 6.0 p.m. and used by much traffic throughout the night. Deep wells with manual deep well pumps found in QUÉANT and HIRONDELLE valley. Fixing these up. QUÉANT sent back to POSIÈRE in Case the of pontoon equipment which had been left there. 2/Lt MORBURN & 416 Fd Co RE and 2 NCO's are attached for liaison. Company moves to C4 central (Map FRANCE 1/20,000 57 c.N.W.) and mounted section to Joinir Coy.	Fine	
C4 central	4th		Fix another forge at QUÉANT. Hand over watching these to 412th Fd Co RE. Work on track as above improving & widening it in morning. In afternoon whole company works on preparing new DH.Q in the HINDENBURG line near QUÉANT. 4 sections stay there the night. Work till dusk. Sick - To Hosp. 1 O.R.	Fine. Thunder watering thunder.	

(35998) Wt. W12859/M1893. 250,000. 1/17. D. D. & L., Ltd. Forms/C.2118-14.

410 (Lowland) Field Co. R.E.

SEPT. 1918

WAR DIARY
or
INTELLIGENCE SUMMARY
(Erase heading not required.)

Army Form C. 2118.

Instructions regarding War Diaries and Intelligence Summaries are contained in F. S. Regs., Part II. and the Staff Manual respectively. Title pages will be prepared in manuscript.

Place	Date	Hour	Summary of Events and Information	Weather	Remarks and references to Appendices
Map FRANCE 1/40,000 67 N.W. Ck central	5th		Woke on new D.H.Q. Section accompanying wagons to camp at Cy central in evening. Pontoon trestle equipment arrive from GROSVILLE.	Showery	
"	6th		Woke on new D.H.Q. & return to Cy central at night.	Very fine.	
B12 B.8.	7th	0800	Moved to B.12 B.8. and made camp. Fixed trough at B.17 & 7.8 and pumps. Trough made at B.12 B.9.81. Odd jobs carpentry job at 155 Bde HQ. Shift Ammo firing huts from new DHQ to present DHQ. Repair pump at Cy central. B sappers to St LEGER to help Engine Coy suppliers to run steam engine at Well there. Forwarded recces recommendations re armed escort attached. Reinf. 2 O.R.	Fine	
"	8th		Made targets. Steam engine ST LEGER. 200 afte units supply fixed on 7'6 trade + fix boxes to supporting targets + levelling for firing points at ranges at B.3 a 4.2 (map 57 N.W) and T.24 d + T.29 a.7.7 (map 57 B.S.W.) Sick - To Hosp. 1 O.R.	Showery	
"	9th		Repaired windows 155 Bde HQ. Bathing + inspection + fixing up to camp. Repair wagons. Rejoined from Hosp. 1 O.R.	"	
"	10th		Bathing. Repair wagons. Making new rifle range for 155 Bde. Officers + 3 N.C.O's here to learning demonstration. Fixing number boards after ranges. Fixing up camp.	"	
"	11th		Training including bombing. Fix trough near 155 Bde HQ. Fix target numbers. Bathing. Reinf. 1 O.R.	"	90.

410th (Lowland) Field Co RE
SEPT 1918

WAR DIARY
or
INTELLIGENCE SUMMARY.
(Erase heading not required.)

Army Form C. 2118.

Place	Date	Hour	Summary of Events and Information	Remarks and references to Appendices
Map FRANCE 1:20,000 57C N.W.	12th	0800	Moved to C.12.c. whole Coy at unknown D.H.Q. in HINDENBURG LINE near QUÉANT. D7a existed (map FRANCE 1:20,000 57C N.E.) Excavating for English shelters. 1 Coy 17th MF(?) also employed on this.	Showery
B12d 8.8 + C12c	13th		Watun D.H.Q. Excavating for and existing shelters. Join in Selnn from QUÉANT. Sick To Hosp. 3. O.R. Reinf. 1.O.R.	Showery.
C12c	14th		as yesterday. Sick To Hosp. 2. O.R.	Showery.
"	15th		" " " 1. O.R.	Fine
"	16th		Reinf. 1.O.R.	Showers night & early but fine showery
"	17th	0730	Work on D.H.Q. Coy H.Q. annexe to D.8.c.3,8 (map of France 1:20,000 Sheet 57C NE) Mounted Section remain at C.12.c.	
Map FRANCE 1:20,000 57C NE	18th	0800	Work on well at C.10.d.2.1. (map of FRANCE 1:20,000 57C N.W.) Taken over from 413 Coy R.E. Remainder of Coy works on D.H.Q. Rejoined from Hospital. 6. O.R.	Very fine night wet
"	19th	0730	Work on well at C.10.d.2.1. completed. Gas proofing Dug outs at Coy. H.Q. Remainder of Coy. working on D.H.Q. Sick To Hosp. 1.O.R. Rejoined from Hosp. 1.O.R.	
"	20th	0730	Coy. working on D.H.Q.	
"	21st	0730	1 Section on 155 Bde. H.Q. in the evening. Dugouts gas proofed at D.9.c.35.15., D9c27.15 D15.a.1.9 D8c.25.83., Remainder Coy on D.H.Q. Rejoined from Hosp. 1.O.R.	Fine
"	22nd	0730	1 Section working on road D9d.4.1.4. D15.a.80. making diversion around crater at D15a02. and filling in shell holes. 1. G.S. limber 1. G.S. waggon employed. 1 Section working on road from D15.B.31 June 40. D.H.Q. 2. G.S. limbers 1 G.S. wagon, Reinf. 8 O.R.	

410th (Lowland) Fld. Coy. R.E.
SEPT. 1918

WAR DIARY
or
INTELLIGENCE SUMMARY
(Erase heading not required.)

Army Form C. 2118.

Place	Date	Hour	Summary of Events and Information	Remarks and references to Appendices
Map of FRANCE 1:20000 57¢ NE	23rd	07.30	1 Section working on road from bridge at D9d.4.1 to D0d.1.6 also improving road up to D.16.c. 1 Section working on road disposal at D.14.a+c. 1 Section encroaching trench equipment. 1 Section working at DHQ. Fine	
	24th	08.00	2 Sections (445 & H) improving roadway & RE widening lattices & Ag/stores. 60 army portee made. Officers reconnoitred Artillery Tracks up to Zond Rd. Map of FRANCE 1-20000 57 NE. Fine Sick - To Hosp. 1 OR	
	25th	07.30	1 Section working forward DHQ at D.H.12.a.6.17. *12mm N° Section found ramps across Junior road at E.25.b.7.9. 4 launch at E.2.6.a.1.9 (the pontoons). N°2 Section - attack if ramped bunker road in E.25.d.35 & the front line at E.22.6.C.1.17. 9 cul with 12 men ramped tatives their two places to 9 GBde RFA. another 12 men improved the alay & track tatives. Back to F.10 a R.7. Sick - To Hosp. 2. O.R. Showery	
	26th	07.30	Intermediate backwards of the same track in E.25.b.6c. * the same track in n DHQ D.28.b.17. Somen pegged out Battalion tracks in E.25.b.6c. 1 Section in n DHQ D.28.b.17. 1 Off. 12 men sacked to Lady. 1 Section improved Track for 9 GBde RFA in J.5.d.6. 1 Section improved road in QUEANT at D.2.c.2.9. One officer party Sick - To - Hosp. 1 OR. Fine,	
			40 men improved road in BOURSIES & LOUVERVAL Area. 1 Section in reserve. 1/C, 412 Fld Coy developed reconnoitred for water in D.22.d.3. and 5.3.6. 1 Section detached under C.E., 412 Fld Coy in reserve at D.8c. 3.8. Coy H.Q. moved to D.22.d.3. and 5.3.6. 1 Section on reserve was made of Canal erete in MOEUVRES. 2 Sections at forward Coy Hq. 1 Section as made of Canal provided Loading parties (materials) at D.1 d 8.0. A reconnaissance was made of Canal	
	27th	05.30	crossing at E.27.c.1.3, the chateau at E.27.d.7.9. 2 Sections moved into MOEUVRES in the evening sand detached under command of 412 Coy RE. Coy Hq moved back to D.8.c.3.8 in evening. Fine Wounded 1. O.R.	

410 (Lowland) Field Coy RE
Sept 1918

WAR DIARY
or
INTELLIGENCE SUMMARY.
(Erase heading not required.)

Army Form C. 2118.

Place	Date	Hour	Summary of Events and Information	Remarks and references to Appendices
Map of FRANCE 1/20,000 57C N.E.	28th	0800	3 Sections detached under orders of O.C. 412 Field Coy RE developed water in MOEUVRES at E14d13, 1,2 & F pump, 1 trough, 6 gallons per horse. E14c 53 1 " 2 " E14c 72 1 " " E20a 78 1 " " were installed. 10 men each / Something huts at Pump and DHQ. D28.b.17 a 84 Traffic signs orders completed. Coy HQ moved to E20.00, on arriving M/d Section regains Coy. 3 Section detached came into water of O.C. 410 Field Coy, on arriving front	
	29th	0900	1 Section on water supply maintenance in MOEUVRES, 2 Section on improved road from E20d96 to E28a 2,0 8 men 16 S wagon 16 S huts worked on road E29a57 & GRAINCOURT. Balance of pontoon equipment at BULLECOURT on moving. All bridging equipment handed over to 63 Div at CANTAING in evening. Showery.	
	30th	0630	1 Section detailed on water near Craves in MOEUVRES. Remainder of Coy + M/d Section moved K.K.2c.3,1 in morning. Reconnaissance made of roads + tracks forward from GRAINCOURT to CANAL DEL'ESCAUT & of wells in GRAINCOURT & ANNEUX	

M Leslie Cap RE
Major R.E.
O.C. 410th (Lowland) Field Coy. R.E.

Confidential

War diary

410th (Lowland)
Field Co RE

Sept 1918

Vol IV No 9

Vol 7

CONFIDENTIAL

WAR DIARY
of
410th (Lowland) Field Coy R.E.
for Period
1st October 1918 To 31st October 1918

Volume — IV No 10

#10 (Railway) Field Co RE ① OCTOBER 1918

WAR DIARY or INTELLIGENCE SUMMARY

Army Form C. 2118.

Instructions regarding War Diaries and Intelligence Summaries are contained in F.S. Regs., Part II. and the Staff Manual respectively. Title pages will be prepared in manuscript.

(Erase heading not required.)

Place	Date	Hour	Weather	Summary of Events and Information	Casualties Reinforcements	Casualties Sick to Hospital	Remarks and references to Appendices
GRAINCOURT	OCTOBER 1.	1300	Fine	Sappers and Tool-carts moved to CANTAING. Transport and H.Q. Personnel within at Graincourt under Lieut. C.B. Dunn. WORKS: Gas proofing D.H.Q. dugouts.			
CANTAING	2.			WORKS: Developing Water Supply from Wells in Cantaing + guard in troughs. Transport awaiting orders for advance.	3 O.R.		
Do.	3		Fine	WORKS: As yesterday. Handed over water equipment at Canal to 413 FLD. CO. R.E. Gas proofing Bde. forward dugouts. New cook house for 155 Bde. Hqrs.		1 O.R. Accidentally injured	
Do.	4.		Fine	WORKS: Water development continuing. No 2 Section attached to K. O.S.B. [Gas proofing continuing] at FAUBOURG de PARIS had been taken.			
Do.	5		Fine	WORKS: As yesterday including making traps for M/Gs.			
Do.	6	0230	Fine AM Rain PM	Company moved to BEAUMETZ-LEZ-CAMBRAI.		1 O.R. Wounded	
BEAUMETZ LES CAMBRAI	7	1430 0900	Fine	Left Beaumetz. Coy. Cambrai Camp, HQ. detrained VADLX VRAUCOURT at 17:30 de do do for LIGNY via GROUVILLE.			
	8.	0530 8/10	Rain do	Arrived LIGNY ST FLANCHEL STATION and detrained. Marched to SARS LE BOIS			
SARS LE BOIS	9		Fair	Bathing + cleaning up stores + equipment.			
Do	10			Training as per programme. No 1 Section Works:— Repairs to tangle at DENIERS. Repairs to tangle at MAGNICOURT. Fixing Troughs + repairs to pumps.			
Do	11			Training as yesterday. No Section Works:— Tangle at Magnicourt also drawing Pontoons + Trestles from DENIERS.	2 O.R.		

410 F (Durham) Field Co RE

WAR DIARY

INTELLIGENCE SUMMARY

(Erase heading not required.)

Army Form C. 2118.

OCTOBER 1918

Place	Date	Hour	Weather	Summary of Events and Information	CASUALTIES REINFORCEMENT	SICK TO HOSPITAL	Remarks and references to Appendices
SARS-LE-BOIS	OCTOBER 12	1600		No.1 Section - Fitting new trestle equipment & cleaning wagons. Making L.G. Targets. Training as yesterday. All S.B.R. tested at BERLENCOURT. Inoculation.			
Do.	13	0800	FAIR.	Rifle Practice on Range at DENIERS. Work Dress with Equipment	1. O.R.		
Do.	14	0900 1500	FINE.	Parade for Divisional R.E. Sports at DENIERS. S.B.R. inspected by Bde. Gas Officer.		1. O.R.	
Do.	15			No.1 Section: Cleaning wagons, equipment & local jobs. Remainder Training as before.		1. O.R.	
Do.	16			All Sappers Training.			
Do.	17			as yesterday.			
Do.	18			Training as yesterday. Draw Pay for Company		1. O.R.	
Do.	19	0800		Move to LIEVIN with 155 Bde. Marched to TINCQUES, entrained for BULLY GRENAY and detrained for LIEVIN. Transport moved by road under Built Huts. Lieut Horrocks.		1. O.R.	
	20			Marched with 155 Bde. to FOUCQUIERES arriving Midday. Moved on to RACHES.			
	21	1330		Marched from RACHES and arrived at DOUAI about 1600 billeted at Barracks. Collecting material for Bridge over Railway on the DOUAI - ORCHIES Road.			
DOUAI	22			Erected trestles for 8 Bay Bridge.	1. O.R. accidentally injured		

H.Q. (Bowland) Field Co. R.E.

WAR DIARY
INTELLIGENCE SUMMARY
(Erase heading not required.)

Army Form C. 2118.

OCTOBER 1918

Place	Date	Hour	Weather	Summary of Events and Information	Casualties Reinforcements	Casualties Sick to Hospital	Remarks and references to Appendices
DOUAI	23	15.20		Working on Bridge up to Noon. 3 + 4 Secs. Carry on afterwards. Traffic down at 20.30. Hd. Qrs. and Nos 1 + 2 Secs. move to MARCHIENNES and billet there about 20.00			
MARCHIENNES	24	15.00		Nos 1 + 2 Secs. Collect material for Bridge over Canal on MARCHIENNES-SOMAIN ROAD. " 3 + 4 " Complete Bridge at DOUAI and join Coy. at MARCHIENNES. Casual works on Marchiennes Bridge. OC AT Coy R.E. decide to erect heavy Bdge on site.		1. O.R.	
do	25			No 1 Sec. Reconstructs bridge over Drain on MARCHIENNES – CATELET ROAD. No 2 " Fill in + construct Road over Gates near ORCHIES. No 3. Resting. No 4 " Move to MILLONFOSSE near ST AMAND under Lt Dunn.			
do	26			No 1 Sec. Complete works in hand near MARCHIENNES. Company moves by road to join No 4 Sec. at MILLONFOSSE. No 4 Sec. Taking out filling and reconstructing Culvert on ORCHIES – ST AMAND road near MILLONFOSSE			
do	27			No 4 Sec as yesterday. Remainder of Sappers on Crib-pier Bridge to be erected over stream near ST AMAND Sty.		2. O.R.	
do	28			No 1 Sec. Resting. 25 R.A. reconstruct wooden ramp to Bridge over Stream at ALENE BOE No 2 + 3. Crib pier bridge at ST AMAND with assistance of 25 R.A. O.R. No 4 Sec. as yesterday with assistance of 25 R.A. other ranks.			
do	29			No 1 Sec. Take up old Culvert on Main Road at ALENE BOE + commence reconstruction. No 2, +3 " as yesterday with R.A. assistance 25 O.R. No 4 " do with R.A. 25 OR.			
do	30	10.00		No 1 Sec. Completed Culvert. 50 R.A. released to Corps RE Dump DOUAI. Nos 2-3+4 Secs. as yesterday each job sharing 25 R.A. personnel. Company moves to billets near LECELLES		1. O.R.	
LECELLES	31			Crib pier Bridge No ST Amand and Culvert near MILLONFOSSE completed No 1. Sec. Cleaning Wagons + equipment			

CONFIDENTIAL

WAR DIARY

410th (Lowland) Field Co. RE

1st - 31st Dec. 1918

Vol IV No 10

CONFIDENTIAL.

WAR DIARY
OF

410th (Lowland) Field Co R.E.

FROM 1/11/1918   TO 30/11/1918

(VOLUME   )

416th (Centaur) Field Coy R.E.

Army Form C. 2118.

WAR DIARY
or
INTELLIGENCE SUMMARY
(Erase heading not required.)

NOVEMBER 1918

Instructions regarding War Diaries and Intelligence Summaries are contained in F.S. Regs., Part II and the Staff Manual respectively. Title pages will be prepared in manuscript.

Place	Date	Hour	Summary of Events and Information	Remarks and references to Appendices
LECELLES	1		Kit inspection. All blacksmiths work on pontoon wagons. Made wooden spin up laddergaff. Casualties 1 O.R. sick	
LECELLES	2		Blacksmiths work on wagons. A/S/mjt seek send 250' camouflage. N.A. 3rd tractor camouflage on wagons. 1 O.R. sent into Ri. nothers heard for APM. Casualties. D.O.R. sick	
"	3		6 Section April 2h N12 Saturday to make Roots to Range from N82 cut nets with hurdles & stakes. N2 1053 Section forming Ladders 10 P4 sold packets sandbags from town. Regimenal. N.A.T.S. Shrapnel Rt.	
"	4		Coy move to LA NEUVILLE EGLISE (J58C2.2.) I58B7. Where moved into Buigde made. Examine report on bridges to N.12 middle to upper 24/h4. Recce survey of along section + outbuilding reasonable for bridges for infantry. DECOURS to PAUL and the DECOURS SCARPE near CHATEAU LABBATE (J20683) + (J23a2.7) by day. War works on bridges all night. Complete DECOURX bridges later before dawn.	MAP LECELLES
LA NEUVILLE EGLISE	5		Officer recce made. Examine reports on site to the Infor tank at MUNSTER. Work on bridges all night. DECOURS bridges 3P16 10ft x 3 trestles. SCARPE bridges by day when work reserves. 420 man hours 16 heavy wagon loads	
"	6		Mens work on ROWEGIES locks with Infantry party called moving. for change bridges Coy on rd. SCARPE bridges and night g. Works enemy from JENNIS from pontoon Park. Casualties 1 O.R. wounded	
"	7		Continue work on RONEGIES tanks. Called at time for work on smokey ground near SCARPE bridges. Parade 6300 for pontooning. Stand down at 0930. J. Sections spent 4/2 forward section & MARCIE JOINVILLE	
"	8		Pontoon orders received. OPAS recce work where enemy has retired. Moeuvres HERGNIES with pontoon equipment. Delayed our movements by water. Recce from ESCAUT + 1 pontoon bridge across CANAL DUSARD at HERGNIES. Pontoons arrive from park + bridge at 1845. 0.R. bridge made up & started at 1900. Recommence work from HERGNIES to MORT DU MERVILLE + LE TRIEN DE HENGNIES to along DE miles around infantry Sport Bn. Co. V Moved to HERGNIES	

WAR DIARY or INTELLIGENCE SUMMARY

Army Form C. 2118.

110th (Scottish) 200 Coy. R.E.

NOVEMBER 1918

Place	Date	Hour	Summary of Events and Information	Remarks and references to Appendices
HERCHIES	9		Small detachment given about 12 I.S.T. Bde. & mats. re-al arched culvert & Railway crossing L/Bc 6.3 near HERCHIES. Coy move to BLATON with 1st Bde. JERUSALEM refs. & pontoon equipment. 1st Bde. & reconnce arriving PLATON. ANTOING–PÉRONNES–BEUIL CANAL. Recon. minor from Bridge ad BUISSIÈRES roads. PÉRONNES. Built bridge for infantry crossing at BLATON (B90961) with eight civilian pontoons; completed after dark; unaccessories. carrier in consequence. Bridge for supply column ad 2nd Lockdam BLATON (B15C 8 a). Stone lorry bridge 6 ton well timbered prep. C5376 open at 2nd lock dam BLATON. Repair broken gd. bridge at CHIMIÈRE road DEFINSART (B20c 3o) with 10" 1 OR sick making with 14th Coy for extra to gd. Roman Road 19/11/18. Casualties: 1 OR sick	ANTOING PÉRONNES CANAL Bridge near Lock No 43 destroyed up to 2 Lockdams MIN 76"
BLATON	10		Strong How bridge at C.9R.91 (PLATON) mounted (11for lorries) & stone road leading up to it. Failure bridge at C82 C8V (PLATON) to suit lorry bridge at B15C89, complete. 100 g mon from 1st No 3 sect. 2 OR wounded at RISQUE to clear away shocks bound	
"	11		Bridges ad G.9R.96 for lorries by 12/15. Bridges ad G.9a 9.1, G.15 C.8.9, G.82 C.8V demolished but with handcarts. Medici brands etc. 2nd 17 Squadds command. Coy3 Second Lgt. forward to SIRAULT. Clear debris from road where military bridge has been demolished at (B (5c66) will contain laborer.	
	12		Coy move to JURBISE. No 3 sect. Supervise work on HERCHIES–SIRAULT road (1 Bn N3 sect working party) Casualties 1 OR sick	
JURBISE	13		No 3 sect supervising work on HERCHIES–SIRAULT road + (8inf Bde. working party). No 2 sect. Coy working party road & by clear killed, unserviceable etc. Post R. etc. road inspection. K10 inspection. Capa on other inspection work Casualties 4 OR sick	
	14		No 3 sect. supervises work on HERCHIES–SIRAULT road (1 battn. working party). Painter painting wagons. Wagon equipment etc. etc. Roads ad Coy & Commander for YSCL & coy air reconnaissance	

WAR DIARY
or
INTELLIGENCE SUMMARY.

Army Form C. 2118.

410th (Lowland) Fd. Coy., R.E.

NOVEMBER 1918

(Erase heading not required.)

Instructions regarding War Diaries and Intelligence Summaries are contained in F. S. Regs., Part II. and the Staff Manual respectively. Title pages will be prepared in manuscript.

Place	Date	Hour	Summary of Events and Information	Remarks and references to Appendices
JURBISE	15		No 3 Sect. superior work on HERCHIES – SIRAULT road (1 Batt. INF. working party) 2 officers & 72 O.R. ground to given date for on formal entry by 1st Army. Remainder Coy. clean wagons. Casualties 2 sick. Reinforcements 2 O.R.	
"	16		Coy inspection full marching order by O.C. No 3 Sect. supervised work on road (as 15.11.18) wash in [?] HERCHIES SIRAULT road. Battle for Coy. training site. Casualties 2 O.R. sick. Reinforcements 1 O.R. from 2/5 hospital	
"	17		Church parade. Casualties 2 O.R. sick	
"	18		Finished main wagons. Remainder of Coy. training. [crossed out] Casualties 1 & T B. modified	
"	19		Parading & cleaning wagons. Remainder of Coy. training	
"	20		Painting & cleaning wagons. Remainder of Coy. training. Casualties 1 O.R. sick. Reinforcements 2 O.R. from [?] hospital	
"	21		CRE inspects Coy. Casualties 3 O.R. sick	
"	22		Joiners made felling letters. Sect. work on wagon poles, pole/pontoon. Finish paint wagons. 2 & sick. Casualties 1 O.R. sick	
"	23		Joiners made latrine seats, seconds for men. Finish paint wagons/pontoon equipment. Remainder of Coy. 2 hrs route march.	
"	24		Church parade. Medical inspection. Casualties 2 O.R. sick. Reinforcements 1 O.R. from 1.B.D. 1 O.R. from [?]	
"	25		No 1 sect. repair pontoon equipment. No 2 sect. clean & repair their equipment. No 3 sect. make & lay mains [?] cook house platters. The Remain. Coy. drill for dismounted men. Reinforcements 1 O.R. from hospital.	Y.I.M.
"	26		Paint wagons. Make latrine seats, grass [?] for D.W.U. No 1 & 4 sect. clean & repair their equipment. 1 O.R. sick [?] Fitzpatrick [?] 3 O.R. joined from hospital. Casualties 1 O.R. sick	

Army Form C. 2118.

WAR DIARY
or
INTELLIGENCE SUMMARY.
(Erase heading not required.)

410th (Lowland) Field Coy R.E.   NOVEMBER 1918

Place	Date	Hour	Summary of Events and Information	Remarks and references to Appendices
JURBISE	27		Coy. inspection by Brigadier 155 Bde. Ceremonial received General Cameron	
JURBISE	28		Paint & clean wagons, make blackboards, mist clapping blocks for S.S.O. Filling latrines. Coy drill & minor fatigues, Nil Casualties 1 O.R. sick	
"	29		Paint & clean wagons, make latrine seats for C.R.E. scaph & impvt stoves trestles etc.	
"	30		Whole Coy route march 2½ hours. Inspected on return by C.R.E. Improvement on date appeared to & explained to men. Casualties 2 O.R. sick.	
			The following were recommended to be named for service in the Field in the Rhine/Belgian warship.
Sapr. John Robt Sanders
Driver/(acpl) George Hamilton Beattie
No 37247 Corporal Robert Hay
" 414014 " Thomas Murray
" 411606 Sapper (a/lce cpl unpaid) Rodrigues
" B7302 " Jacob Wright
" 414083 Driver Thomas Findlay
" 414437 Sapper William Hector
" 411583 " William Russell Nelson
" 414187 " Gilbert Thomson
" 414563 " Andrew Miller
" 36966 Sergeant Charles Moote
" 411602 2/Cpl James Hardwick
" 414190 " John Bowman	OP Peter Major R.E. OC 410 FdCo 1.12.18

989

CONFIDENTIAL.

WAR DIARY

OF

410th (Lowland) Field Co. R.E.

FROM 1st December, 1918. TO 31st December, 1918.

(VOLUME   )

December 1918 — WAR DIARY or INTELLIGENCE SUMMARY

410th (Lowland) Field Coy. R.E.   Army Form C. 2118.

Place	Date	Hour	Summary of Events and Information	Remarks and references to Appendices
JURBISE (BELGIUM)	1/12/18		Erected weather shingle.	
"	2/12/18		Carpentry work. Cleaning & painting pontoons. Casualties:- 1 O.R. sick to hospital. Reinforcements:- 1 O.R. from Base. 1 O.R. gained from hospital.	
"	3/12/18		Carpentry work. Cleaning & painting pontoons. Troops passing through District Reinforcements:- 1 O.R. from Base. 1 O.R. gained from hospital.	
"	4/12/18		Carpentry work. Cleaning & painting pontoon equipment. Troops passing through winter from MONS.	
"	5/12/18		Carpentry work. Cleaning & painting pontoon equipment. Troops wagon park. Casualties:- 1 O.R. sick to hospital. Units from MONS.	
"	6/12/18		Carpentry work. Cleaning & renewing pontoon equipment. Repairing communication & Bengola range.	
"	7/12/18		Carpentry work. Cleaning & renewing pontoon equipment. Repairing communication & Bn. rifle range.	
"	8/12/18		Church parade. Casualties:- 2 O.R. sick to hospital.	
"	9/12/18		Carpentry work. Clearing wagons & completing roots. Repairing & construction Rifle range. Casualties:- 1 O.R. sick to hospital. Reinforcements:- 2 O.R. gained from hospital.	
"	10/12/18		Carpentry work. Cleaning & renewing pontoon equipment. Repairing con. services & Bn. rifle range. Reinforcements:- 1 O.R. gained from hospital.	
"	11/12/18		Carpentry work. Making & painting traffic signs. Renewing pontoon equipment. Supervising construction of Bn. rifle range.	
"	12/12/18		Carpentry work. Making & painting traffic signs. Renewing pontoon equipment. Painting & erecting Sign Boards. Supervising construction of light range & making target frames. Casualties:- 2 O.R. sick to hospital.	
JURBISE	13/12/18	1000	Coy. moved to LENS (BELGIUM) arriving at successive Bn. rifle range. Work on salvage. Coy. went out taking up work and painting Signs. Casualties: 1 O.R. sick to hospital.	
LENS (BELGIUM)	14/12/18		Work of salvage etc. Nos. 1 and 3 little Nos. Sections getting can. Family going line equipment etc. Casualties:- 1 O.R. sick to hospital. Reinforcements:- 1 O.R. gained from hospital.	

December 1918   **WAR DIARY**   410th (Durham) Fld. Coy. R.E.   Army Form C. 2118.

or

INTELLIGENCE SUMMARY.

(Erase heading not required.)

Instructions regarding War Diaries and Intelligence Summaries are contained in F. S. Regs., Part II. and the Staff Manual respectively. Title pages will be prepared in manuscript.

Place	Date	Hour	Summary of Events and Information	Remarks and references to Appendices
LENS (BELGIUM)	15/12/18		Tours of settlement, entrances etc. for new billets. Casualties :- 3 O.R. sick to hospital	
"	16/12/18		Carpentry work. Painting traffic signs. Vocational cycles. Educational classes. Reinforcements :- 5 O.R. from Base.	
"	17/12/18		G.O.C.'s Inspection. Reinforcements :- LT.B. Munship 2nd Army from hospital	
"	18/12/18		Carpentry work. Making & painting traffic signs. Vocational cycles. Educational classes. Casualties : 1 OR sick to hospital.	
"	19/12/18		Carpentry work. Making & painting traffic signs. Painting cycles. Educational classes	
"	20/12/18		Carpenters work. Making & painting traffic signs. Educational classes. Wagons transported to Mills to be turned & fitted for civilians. Reinforcements :- 1 O.R. transferred from L.R. Fld. Coy. R.E.	
"	21/12/18		Carpentry work. Making & painting traffic signs. Tripods with rope & tackle made at Mills & M.N.T. for civilians. Educational classes. Casualties :- 1 O.R. sick to hospital. Reinforcements :- 1 O.R. from 75 Field Coy. R.E.	
"	22/12/18		Church parade. Reinforcements :- 1 OR joined from hospital	
"	23/12/18		Carpenters work. Making & painting traffic signs. Casualties :- 1 OR sick to hospital. Reinforcements L.R. joined from hospital.	
"	24/12/18		Carpenters work. Materials & painting traffic signs. Tripods & wagon destined to Pusan Mills & M.N.T. for civilians. Educational classes. Reinforcements :- 1 O.R. from Base.	
"	25/12/18		Xmas Day. Casualties :- 1 O.R. sick to hospital.	
"	26/12/18		Carpentry work. Making & painting traffic signs. Educational classes. Casualties : 1 O.R. sick to hospital. Reinforcements :- 1 L.R. joined from hospital.	
"	27/12/18		Carpenters work. Painting traffic signs. G.S. wagons taken & Belgian Refugees transferred to MONS. Educational classes.	
"	28/12/18		Carpentry work. Painting signs. G.S. wagon to DN.I. Belgian Refugees to MONS. Educational classes. Casualties : 1 OR sick to hospital. Reinforcements :- 1 OR joined from hospital.	
"	29/12/18		Church parade. Wagon taking Belgian Refugees to MONS. Casualties :- 1 OR sick to hospital. Reinforcements : 1 OR joined from hospital.	
"	30/12/18		Carpentry work. Getting and painting signs. Signs. Educational classes	
"	31/12/18		Carpentry work. Getting and painting signs for the new Educational classes. Wagons taking men to their billets at MNL. 7 Esplanade. 2 OR reported sick from hospital	

Qualm Maj R.E.
O.C. 410 Fld Coy R.E. 4th

31.12.18

410 Fuld
Roy R.
Van Drang
December
1918

CONFIDENTIAL

WAR DIARY

OF

410ᵗʰ (LOWLAND) FIELD COMPANY R.E.

FROM Jan 1st. 1919.   TO Jan 31st. 1919.

(VOLUME   )

Army Form C. 2118.

WAR DIARY or INTELLIGENCE SUMMARY.

(Erase heading not required.)

JANUARY 1919 410 LOWLAND FIELD COY RE

Instructions regarding War Diaries and Intelligence Summaries are contained in F.S. Regs., Part II. and the Staff Manual respectively. Title pages will be prepared in manuscript.

Place	Date	Hour	Summary of Events and Information	Remarks and references to Appendices
LENS (BELGIUM)	1/1/19		New Years Day	
"	2/1/19		Carpentry Work. Improvements to Billets. Inspection & Classification of all Coy horses. Medical Inspection of men with Readability form. Education Classes	Reinforcements 4 O.R. from R.E.B.D. Rouen
"	3/1/19		Carpentry Work. Trestle Cyps. Returns to Inframmerie. 6 Horses, cutting road for exchange. Education Classes. Improvements to Billets.	Attached for Duty:- 1 Lt H.G. Bloore RE Trestle Wagon with lock timber from Hons. 2 O.R. Left Unit for Courses. 2 O.R. Reinforcements. 1 Officer & 1 O.R. from Hospital.
"	4/1/19		Carpentry Work in Community. Improvements to Billets.	Under N.C.O. scale for inlying. Education Classes.
"	5/1/19		Church Parade. Classes at Billet area (1 hour)	2 O.R. from Hospital. 1 Officer & 1 O.R. from Course. R.E.B.D. 2 O.R. Left for Demobilization.
"	6/1/19		Carpentry 1 & 2 at Community. Trestle timber fetched and for 2 trestles. Bridge Panels. Education Classes.	Reinforcements - 3 O.R. Casualties :- 1 O.R.
"	7/1/19		Coy marched to Justine for Inspection by Brigadier.	Reinforcements. 2 O.R. reported from hospital.
"	8/1/19		Carpentry Work. Fixing up Electric Light. Ergin at R.H.2. Trestle timber fetched. Trestle Wagon like repairs in Camp. Removal of left barrels for Canadians for translation	Trestles by G.O.R. 62 Ars at Justice. 2 men sent by Lieut. M.M. To Tournai & Erivan Lanlin.
"	9/1/19		Carpentry Work. Battle at Justice. Improvements to Billets. Badian in demobilization. Clearing of Billet area. Command stalls at Justice.	
"	10/1/19		Carpentry Work. Battle of Justice. Plugin. Electric Light at R.H.2. Improvements to Billets. Return Readability. Men attached from H.Q.C. 152 Medical Ability inspected by M.O. Education Classes.	Left for Demobilization. 6 O.R.
"	11/1/19		Carpentry Works. Battle at Justice. Electric Light at R.H.2. Improvements to Billets. Erecting Gymnastic apparatus.	Left for Demobilization. 3 O.R.
"	12/1/19		Carpentry Work. Battle at Justice. Gis work for Gas Tram. Education Classes.	9/1/19 Reinforcements:- 4 O.R. from R.E.B.D. Demobilization 1 O.R.
"	13/1/19		Carpentry Work. Battle at Justice. D.H.2 Rigging kit. Erecting Gymnastic apparatus. Education Classes.	Left for Demobilization. 3 O.R.
"	14/1/19		Carpentry Work. Battle at Justice. D.H.2 Rigging kit. Erecting Gymnastic Apparatus. Coy leaving in Cow of Horses. Education Classes. Roll of Horses.	Left for Demobilization. 1 Officer & 6 O.R.
"	15/1/19		Carpentry Work. Battle at Justice. D.H.2 Rigging kit. Improvements to Billets. Inspection of Mares leaving for England. Education Classes.	Left for Demobilization. 2 O.R.

WAR DIARY 410th (LOWLAND) FIELD COY R.E. Army Form C. 2118.

JANUARY 1919

INTELLIGENCE SUMMARY.

(Erase heading not required)

(2)

Place	Date	Hour	Summary of Events and Information	Remarks and references to Appendices
LENS (BELGIUM)	16/1/19		Carpentry Work. Carting Coal for Civilians. Remainder of Coy proceeded to BATTLEFIELD OF WATERLOO on 2 Motor Lorries. Educational Trip.	
"	17/1/19		Carpentry Work. Billet Improvements. Carting Coal & Wood for Civilians. Education Classes	
"	18/1/19		Carpentry Work. Carting Coal for Civilians. Divisional Ceremonial Parade for Presentation of Ribbons by Corps Commander	
"	19/1/19		Church Parade. Clean Billet Area (1 Hour) REINFORCEMENTS 1 O R FROM HOSPITAL	
"	20/1/19		No Work. 52nd Low R.E. Sports. CLASSIFICATION OF 10 HORSES. LEFT FOR DEMOBILIZATION — 5 O R	
"	21/1/19		Carpentry Work. Billet Improvements. Education Classes. Erecting Basket ball & other Baths. Carting for Civilians. LEFT FOR DEMOBILIZATION :- 5 O R	
"	22/1/19		Carpentry Work. Billet Improvements. Education Classes. Erecting Platform Justice Hall. Carting for Civilians	
"	23/1/19		Carpentry Work. Billet Improvements. Education Classes. Erecting Platform Justice Hall. Carting for Civilians	
"	24/1/19		Carpentry Work. Billet Improvements. Education Classes. Erecting Platform Justice Hall	
"	25/1/19		Carpentry Work. Education Classes. Justice Baths. Work for R.E. Sports	
"	26/1/19		Church Parade	
"	27/1/19		Carpentry Work. Billet Improvements. Education Classes. REINFORCEMENT 1 O R FROM HOSPITAL DEMOBILIZED AN ENGLAND 1 O R	
"	28/1/19		Billet Improvements. Civilian Hand Outlets. Education Classes. Carting for Civilians. 2 O R FROM COURSES	
"	29/1/19		Education Classes. Billet Improvements. LEFT FOR DEMOBILIZATION :- 11 O R	
"	30/1/19		Education Classes. Billet Improvements.	
"	31/1/19		Education Classes. Carpentry work. Billet Improvements.	

Philip Majnke
O/C 410 Fld Coy R.E.
1.2.19

410 2nd Coy
9/11

CONFIDENTIAL.

WAR DIARY.

FEBRUARY 1919.

FEBRUARY 1919 **WAR DIARY** 410 (Lowland) FIELD COY. Army Form C. 2118.
R.E.

or

INTELLIGENCE SUMMARY.

(Erase heading not required.)

Place	Date	Hour	Summary of Events and Information	Remarks and references to Appendices
LENS (BELGIUM)	1.2.19		Carpentry work, manufacture of appliances for Bn. Sports, baths etc. Blr. Rds. over latrines etc. N°2 Beer baths sunday & wednesday. A.O.IV a(11011)118. SBR left unit for demob. 16R. rejoined. Lt. G.I. Medforth left for D.of E. Stores VERTON.	
	2.2.19		2 Lorry at DIDO took part. BRUXELS. 5 O.R. left unit for demob. 1 O.R. reinforcement from G.B.D.	
	3.2.19		Carpentry work, Bunkshafe appliances to Dil Spots. Education classes. Improvement of billets. N°2 Beer baths Sunday. Boxing Platform TURBISE. 4 horses lent to civilians. 4 O.R. left unit for demob.	
	4.2.19		Coy wagons inspected by O.C. Carpenters work. Dil Spots gear. Bd. Doors. Boxing platform at JURBISE. 1 Khaki wagon load of timber brought from Canal dump Pit Bois shet 45 H/40000	
	5.2.19		Map 1/BG 26NW, field FRANCE. Carpentry. Dil Spots appliances. Bd. new Education classes. Officers inspected hut at ERBISOEUL. Section baths. Major G. Stewart left unit to take over C.R.E. 52nd Div. Capt. G.H. Beattie takes over command of 410th (Low) Field Coy. R.E.	
	6.2.19		Carpentry. Dil Spots gear. Repair storms board for boxing ring TURBISE. 1 section baths.	
	7.2.19		Coy wagons cleaned. 3 O.R. left unit for demob. Coy Kits inspected. Carpenters on Dil Spots gear. 1 Section baths. Dud Shells at CAMBRON St VINCENT inspected. 6 O.R. left unit for demob. Lt. H.G. Bloore returned to 413 (Low) Field Coy. R.E.	
	8.2.19		Boxing platform at JURBISE dismantled & moved to Coy dump LENS. Shells investigated at CAMBRON St VINCENT. Mid Section baths. 9 O.R. left unit for demob.	
	9.2.19		2 L mis. took part to BRUXELS. 6 O.R. left unit for demob.	
	10.2.19		Carpentry. 2 cycles & 1/2 horse of garage. Ladders made. Bath gauge at JURBISE battle played. 6 O.R. left unit for demob. "Lt. G.I. Medforth returned to unit from D.of E. Stores VERTON.	
	11.2.19		1 cloth horse etc. put in the dismantled & returned to Coy Dump from Lorries. Layout. 3 O.R. Returned from garage of carpentry to own unit.	
	12.2.19		Carpentry. Horse watering trough repaired. Tool carts overhauled. Slate sharpened.	

WAR DIARY or INTELLIGENCE SUMMARY

Army Form C. 2118.

FEBRUARY 410 (Lowland) FIELD COY R.E.

Place	Date	Hour	Summary of Events and Information	Remarks and references to Appendices
LENS (BELGIUM)	13.2.19		Carpentry. Bed fixed in Lamers store. Sandbags hutting trenched. Spare Lamers checked & logged	
	14.2.19		On wagons cleaned & logged. AF Z18 filled up the men of Coy. Spr G.T. Mudforth left unit for demob.	
	15.2.19		Spare Lamers cleaned & logged. 6 Sappers to stables to make room for horses. Railway accommodation for shells between LENS & CAMBRAIN-CASTEAU	
	16.2.19		Church service. Optional	
	17.2.19		4 men cleaning & laying Lamers. Repairs to 6th H.L.I. Range at V2 4c 7.2. Spr 38 1/40070 dismantled material returned to Coy dump LENS. 2 beds made for horses	
	18.2.19		Range at V2 4c 7.2. dismantled. 4 Sappers laying Lamers. Repairs to 6th H.L.I. billets. 1 OR to hospital accidentally injured. 1 OR returned from leave to UK. 2 motor crates for MGC	
	19.2.19		do — 1 Lecture Battle, 2 motor crates for MGC	
	20.2.19		Depression in stable attached ??? to the wagons made. Repairs to 6th H.L.I. billets. 8 Sappers stacking trellis at the Stables. 2 crates for MGC completed	
	21.2.19		2 trestles + 2 large carpentering loaded up on cattle wagon. Carpenters table for 52 DW reception camp. 1 OR returned from leave to UK.	
	22.2.19		Dismantling carried out V2 4 C 7.2. Supervised. Work at 6th H.L.I. completed. Shifting equipment checked. 1 OR demobilised whilst on leave in UK. Church parade.	
	23.2.19		Carpenters table for 52 = DW Reception Camp. Remainder of Coy erecting racecourse stand + jumps on K.9.b.8.2. Map of BELGIUM & part of FRANCE sheet 44S Scale 1/40000	
	26.2.19		do do	
	27.2.19		Coy went in lorry to copse. Races at K.9.b. central 1 NCO & 13 men repaired jumps between races. 2 OR left unit for demob. 1 OR transferred to "WATFORD DETAILS".	
	28.2.19		Coy went in lorry to Corps races held at K.9.b central 1 NCO & 13 men repaired jumps between races. JMB	

J M Beater Capt RE
OC 410 Low Field Coy RE

4/10 Fld Co Rly
Vol 12

CONFIDENTIAL

WAR DIARY

MARCH 1919.

WAR DIARY of 410th LOWLAND FIELD COY, RE Army Form C. 2118.
or INTELLIGENCE SUMMARY.
MARCH

Place	Date	Hour	Summary of Events and Information	Remarks and references to Appendices
LENS (BELGIUM)	1.3.19		Carpentry work on Billet (Orderly Room)	
	2.3.19		Sunday. No work.	
	3.3.19		Carpentry work on Billet as above. Cleaning Coy Wagons. 2 N.C.O's & 3 Men checking Machinery & Engines with Lt Borrington.	
	4.5.19		Carpentry work as above. Checking Machinery at Engines as above. Bradley & 2 N.C.O's for Machine Gun Battn at Carvin St Vincent to arrange 3 men checking Machinery & Engines. Cleaning Coy wagons & sectionising equipment at Queen siding. CASUALTIES:- 1 OR to HOSPITAL	
	5.3.19		Work as above.	
	6.3.19		Lt Borrington & party at Engines. Lorry to take remainder of men to Brussels. CASUALTIES 1 OR TRANSFERRED TO 20 T.F DEPOT	
	7.3.19		Lt Borrington. Party at Engines. Work on Ressources Shed. Cleaning Wagons. Men Bathing.	
	8.3.19		Overhauling No 1. Sector Tool Cart. Carpenters making box. Remainder on wagons cleaning and painting. CASUALTIES:- 1 OR to HOSPITAL	
	9.3.19		Sunday. No CHURCH PARADE. No Work. REINFORCEMENTS:- 1 OR FROM HOSPITAL	
	10.3.19		Lorry to take men to mess. Sent off 2 Trestle Wagons with superstructure for shed at Ressources Carpenters on box.	
	11.3.19		Pushing Wagon Park at Engines. Carpenters finishing box. Cleaning & Sharpening Tools. Cleaning Wagons.	
	12.3.19		Pushing Wagon Park at Engines. Tool teams brought tools superstructures from Ressources. Cleaning Tools & Leather Work.	
	13.3.19		Work as above. Cleaning Tools & Leather Work of Tool Carts. Cleaning Wagons.	
	14.3.19		do. Cleaning & Sharpening Tools. Medical Inspection of coy. CASUALTIES:- 4 OR's FOR DEMOBILIZATION	
	15.3.19		Cleaning of Stables. Cleaning & Sharpening Tools. Cleaning Wagons. Bombardier Coy Kewkesti 1 Section Bathed. DECORATIONS: 414439 Sjt Hector W annuel MEDAILLE BARBATIE Ci CREDINTA 3rd CLASS (Roumanian)	
	16.3.19		Sunday. No Parade. REINFORCEMENTS:- 1 OR FROM HOSPITAL	
	17.3.19		Cleaned & Bogged Stone Harrow. Loaded & cleaned Pontoon Trestle Wagon equipment. CASUALTIES:- 1 OR OFF STRENGTH	
	18.3.19		do. Cleaned Wagons. Recommenced Billet at Engines.	

WAR DIARY of 440th LOWLAND FIELD COY R.E.

INTELLIGENCE SUMMARY

Army Form C. 2118.

MARCH (2)

Place	Date	Hour	Summary of Events and Information	Remarks and references to Appendices
LENS (BELGIUM)	19.3.19		Horses (6 Nos) handed in to Remounts. CASUALTIES:- 9 O.R. FOR DEMOBILIZATION. DRAFT OF 28 O.R'S CONDUCTED BY 2/LIEUT BOVINGTON PROCEEDED TO 90th FIELD COY R.E. ARMY OF OCCUPATION. 1 OFFICER STRUCK OFF STRENGTH (MAJOR STREETEN) CASUALTIES:- 1 O.R. PROCEEDED TO 90th FIELD COY R.E. A of O. 1 O.R. STRUCK OFF STRENGTH.	
	20.3.19		Dismantling Hut at Justice. do	
	21.3.19		Coy PACKING UP. LATRINES LIFTED. BILLETING BOARDS COLLECTED. COY PROCEEDED TO SOIGNIES 1 O.R. STRUCK OFF STRENGTH. (U.K.)	
SOIGNIES (BELGIUM)	22.3.19		Settling down. Billets. Fixing up Wagon Park.	
	24.3.19		Loaded up & brought 3 lorries material from Roeulx bus. Work on building.	
	25.3.19		Handed Bicycles into Ordnance. Builded & closed counter arrant. Work on Horses. CASUALTIES: 1 OFFICER (2/LIEUT BOVINGTON) noted G 552 (AT) COY R.E.	
	26.3.19		Work on Horses	
	27.3.19		do. Fixing up Baths for Coy. Making ramps for entraining purposes CASUALTIES:- 2 O.R. FOR DEMOBILIZATION.	
	28.3.19		do. Coy Bathed. Work on Ramps.	
	29.3.19		do. Work on Ramps & Bridge for entraining purposes	
	30.3.19		Sunday No Work	
	31.3.19		Work on Ramps & Bridges	

M Wheatter Capt MCE
OC 410 Low Field Coy RE

CONFIDENTIAL

410 Fd Coy
Vol 13

WAR DIARY.

for APRIL 1919.

H. Hellewell Lieut RE
O.C. 410th (Lowland) Field Co. R.E.

WAR DIARY or INTELLIGENCE SUMMARY

Army Form C. 2118.

Place	Date	Hour	Summary of Events and Information	Remarks and references to Appendices
Soignies	1/4/19		Loaded up all Ammunition & Explosives at Wagon Park. 200 Carpenters engaged on making Packing Cases to Cary Company Equipment Canvas etc	
	2/4/19		Bakery Parade at 08.45 a.m. Carpenters making Packing Cases for Coy Equipment	
	3/4/19		Carpenters engaged on making Packing Cases for Company Equipment	
	4/4/19			
	5/4/19		Church Parade	
	6/4/19		Reported on Sprg Baths at 111 Loss Fld Ambulance & made reference to same	
	7/4/19		Removed Sprg Baths from Gueture to Soignies	
	8/4/19		All Carpenters making Packing Cases for Coy Equipment. Placed Boiler at 111 Loss Field Ambulance	
	9/4/19		Cleaning Packing Vans. Carpenters making Packing Cases. R/E Inspection	
	10/4/19		Cleaning Packing Wagons	
	11/4/19		Cleaning Packing Wagons. Packing H.Q. Equipment & Vanning out Packing Cases	
	12/4/19		Church Parade	
	13/4/19		Water taps at Signal Os ready Room (53 Rue de la Station). Making a new Cook house	
	14/4/19		Carpenters, Water taps and Cleaning & Vanning Wagons	
	15/4/19		Completed new Cook house. Army & Water Cart. Carpenters working on Packing Cases	
	16/4/19		Cleaning & Painting G.S Wagon & Water Cart	
	17/4/19			
	18/4/19			
	19/4/19		Church Parade	
	20/4/19		Holiday	
	21/4/19		Making inventory of contents of Packing Cases. Painting & Cleaning Wagons	
	22/4/19			
	23/4/19		Cleaning & Painting Wagons	
	24/4/19			
	25/4/19		Bakery Parade 0900	

Army Form C. 2118.

WAR DIARY
or
INTELLIGENCE SUMMARY.
(Erase heading not required.)

Instructions regarding War Diaries and Intelligence Summaries are contained in F. S. Regs., Part II. and the Staff Manual respectively. Title pages will be prepared in manuscript.

Place	Date	Hour	Summary of Events and Information	Remarks and references to Appendices
Sorignies	26/4/19		Church parade. Wagons. Motor repairs at Divisional Bath.	
	27/4/19		Church Parade	
	28/4/19			
	29/4/19		Army & oiling wagons	
	30/4/19		Pay Parade 1.00	

H. Hellewell
Lieut R.E.
O.C. 410th (Lowland) Field Co. R.E.

CONFIDENTIAL

War Diary

410 FD Co. R.E.

Month of

April 1919

WR 14
cover

410th (LOWLAND) FIELD COY R.E.

— WAR DIARY —

— MAY 1919 —

Army Form C. 2118.

WAR DIARY
or
INTELLIGENCE SUMMARY

410th (Low) FIELD Coy R.E.

(Erase heading not required.)

Instructions regarding War Diaries and Intelligence Summaries are contained in F. S. Regs., Part II. and the Staff Manual respectively. Title pages will be prepared in manuscript.

Place	Date	Hour	Summary of Events and Information	Remarks and references to Appendices
SOIGNIES	1-5-19 to 31-5-19		The Coy. is engaged in cleaning & painting Coy wagons, overhauling Coy equipment & in Sports.	
			J.M. Heather Capt RE O.C. 410 (Low) Field Coy R.E.	

Casualties for Month of May 1919.

	Sick to Hospital.		On Leave to U.K.		Returned from Leave.	
	Officers	O.R.	Officers	O.R.	Officers	O.R.
410th. Fd. Coy. R.E.	1	2	1	7	2	2

www.ingramcontent.com/pod-product-compliance
Lightning Source LLC
Chambersburg PA
CBHW081448160426
43193CB00013B/2414